Understanding Money
Earning Money
Revised Edition

Nick Hunter

Heinemann Library
Chicago, Illinois

www.capstonepub.com
Visit our website to find out more information about Heinemann-Raintree books.

To order:
☎ Phone 800-747-4992
🖥 Visit www.capstonepub.com to browse our catalog and order online.

©2012, 2022 Heinemann Library
an imprint of Capstone Global Library, LLC
Chicago, Illinois

All rights reserved. No part of this publication may be reproduced or transmitted in any form or by any means, electronic or mechanical, including photocopying, recording, taping, or any information storage and retrieval system, without permission in writing from the publisher.

Edited by Megan Cotugno
Designed by Ryan Frieson
Original illustrations © Capstone Global Library, Ltd.
Illustrated by Planman Technologies
Picture research by Mica Brancic
Originated by Capstone Global Library, Ltd.

Library of Congress Cataloging-in-Publication Data is available on the Library of Congress website.
ISBN 9781484683163 (paperback)
ISBN 9781484683118 (kindle KF8)

Acknowledgments

The author and publishers are grateful to the following for permission to reproduce copyright material: agefotostock: Jose Fuste Raga, 33; Alamy: Golden Pixels LLC, 36, Jon Arnold Images Ltd, 18; Getty Images: Andy Aitchison, 17, Bettmann, 10, 35, Fuse, 6, 23, Gerard SIOEN, 8, Hulton-Deutsch, 11, 14, Image Source, 15, Michael Ochs Archives, 31, Monty Rakusen, cover, Rune Hellestad, 43, Rykoff Collection, 13; Newscom: Reuters/Kimberly White, 21, SUSANA GONZALEZ/picture-alliance, 42; Shutterstock Premier: Gianni Dagli Orti, 9, The Art Archive, 12; Shutterstock: Artifan, 39, Chekyravaa, 26, Dragana Gordic, 41, Lein de León Yong, 25, Monkey Business Images, 28, Panumas Yanuthai, 40, paul prescott, 19, Zhao jiankang, 4

We would like to thank Michael Miller for his invaluable help in the preparation of this book.

Every effort has been made to contact copyright holders of any material reproduced in this book. Any omissions will be rectified in subsequent printings if notice is given to the publisher.

All the Internet addresses (URLs) given in this book were valid at the time of going to press. However, due to the dynamic nature of the Internet, some addresses may have changed, or sites may have changed or ceased to exist since publication. While the author and Publishers regret any inconvenience this may cause readers, no responsibility for any such changes can be accepted by either the author or the Publishers.

Contents

What Is the Economy?	4
Why Do People Need to Earn Money?	6
Has the Way that People Earn Money Changed?	8
What Has Changed Since 1900?	14
How Do People Earn Money Now?	16
Who Works in Services?	22
How Do Public Workers Earn Money?	28
Does Everyone Work for Someone Else?	30
Who Decides How Much People Earn?	32
What Happens When People Can't Earn Money?	34
Why Does All This Matter to Me?	38
In Focus: Who Are the Richest People in the World?	42
Money Facts	44
Glossary	46
Find Out More	47
Index	48

You can find the answers to the Solve It! questions on page 45.

Some words are shown in bold, **like this**. You can find out what they mean by looking in the glossary on page 46.

What Is the Economy?

If you ask someone what the economy is, that person will normally say it is all about money. That is partly true, but it is nowhere near the whole story.

An economy is the total of all the **wealth** created in a society. Wealth does not just mean money. It also includes goods and services that are made by human work. Goods are things that are made, sold, and purchased. Services are things that one person pays another person to do. Most goods and services we use or need are created by work. Food is grown and then prepared for us to eat. Machines like cars are made in a factory. Even music is created by the work of a musician.

Consumers and workers are often the same people. Workers use the money they earn to buy products.

Sometimes we talk about the world economy, which includes all the wealth created in the world. We might also talk about the economy of our own country, which is linked to the world economy in many ways. You could even think of each household as a small economy.

Parts of an economy

There are three key parts of an economy that we need to understand:

- **Consumers**: These are the people who buy and use goods and services to meet their needs, whether those are basic needs such as food, or luxuries like the latest designer clothes. We are all consumers.

- Workers: These are the people who make the products the consumers need. They usually get paid money in return for their work.

- Business owners or **capitalists**: These are the people who own businesses and employ workers. They **invest** money in order to make more money, or **profit**.

Our economy is called a capitalist economy. This chart shows the links between owners, workers and consumers. Other key parts of the economy are banks and governments.

Why Do People Need to Earn Money?

If you get an allowance or earn money yourself, you use that money to buy things. You might choose to buy things for yourself or presents for your friends. If you did not have that money, you would not be able to buy anything.

Most of the things we need to live our lives cost money. Some goods and services are essential, or necessary for life. Each family has to buy food and drinks. Electricity and water services need to be paid for. People need to earn money to pay for these essential things.

The biggest single thing people have to pay for is usually the place where they live.

Other things are not quite so important. Some of us like to buy new clothes, the latest cell phone, or go on vacation. Whether we can afford to buy all the things we want depends on how much money we earn. Most of us have to make choices about which things are most important to spend our money on.

Paying taxes

Other services we use, like roads and schools, also cost money to build and run. We do not normally pay for these directly. Some of the money we earn goes to the government to pay for these essential public services. This money is called tax.

Solve It!

Your budget

The amount of money you have to spend is your **budget**. Make a list of what you spend each week on different things. What are the essential items and what are the things that you could do without?

MY WEEKLY BUDGET

Income

Allowance	$9
Money earned from washing cars	$9
Total income	$18

Fixed expenses

Cell phone costs	$6
Savings	$5

Other expenses

Snacks and drinks	$5
Magazines	$3
Total spending	$19

Has the Way that People Earn Money Changed?

In the earliest times, people would hunt animals and gather wild plants to provide for their basic needs. Once humans learned how to grow crops, a system of exchanges, or **barters**, started. Hunters would exchange the animals they caught for crops grown by the farmers. As societies became more complex and more goods were bartered, this system did not work as well. Societies began to develop money as something that everyone could recognize as having **value** (worth) for exchanges.

Workers in Ancient Egypt did not receive money. They would spend part of the year working for the pharaoh (ruler) and would receive food from the royal stores in return.

Earning money in ancient times

In ancient civilizations, most people were not **employed** by someone else who paid them money in return for their work. Most people worked for themselves and sold what they produced to earn money. This was true whether they were a farmer growing wheat and selling it, or a baker who bought the wheat, made bread, and sold it. Businesses that required a large number of workers would often use **slaves**, who were bought and sold themselves, rather than paying people to work for them.

In societies like Ancient Greece and Rome, many people lived in cities. Specialist jobs started to develop, such as craftspeople making fine clothes and jewelry. During the **medieval** period, these craftspeople were organized into official **guilds** to ensure quality work and protect their rights.

Skilled craftsmen and traders like this cloth merchant organized themselves into guilds.

The feudal system

In medieval Europe, many people outside the cities farmed land that was owned by the local lord. A proportion, or part, of the crops they grew was given to the lord. The lord could sell these crops to earn money and pay for things like building castles and fighting wars. In return, the lord would protect the people who farmed the land. This was called the **feudal system**.

Over time, farming methods improved. This meant that fewer people had to work on the land and more food was produced that could be sold. This led to new ways of earning money, too. New **industries** began to develop.

Merchants and trade

New inventions also changed how money could be earned. Ships could sail to far off lands to find goods like pepper and spices. **Merchants** could make a lot of money selling these goods, but it was risky. If the ship was lost at sea, they could lose everything.

For 200 years, slaves were taken against their will from Africa to colonial America. They worked on **plantations** growing crops like cotton. Traders and plantation owners earned money by trading and using slave labor.

Adam Smith (1723–1790)

Adam Smith was born in Kirkcaldy, Scotland. His book *The Wealth of Nations* (1776) included many new ideas about earning money and the world of work. He worked out that large factories could produce more goods than small workshops. If the tasks involved in making something were each done by different workers, this would produce more than if each worker was doing all the tasks involved. Smith's ideas about how work should be organized were the basis for how we earn money today.

Factories changed where people lived as well as how they earned money. New cities grew up around the new factories.

Industrial Revolution

From the mid-1700s, major changes took place in the way people earned money. This time of change was called the **Industrial Revolution**. It happened first in Britain, followed by other European countries, North America, and Japan. New technologies such as steam power and powerful machines for spinning and weaving cloth meant that many more goods could be produced more quickly.

To use these new machines, people had to work in large factories. Setting up these factories and paying the workers required large amounts of money, or capital. This was the start of the **capitalist** system we have today.

The first industrial workers worked long hours in dangerous and dirty conditions. They would often work seven days a week. Over time, laws were introduced to protect workers and stop employers from using children as workers.

Moving to cities

Even after the Industrial Revolution, not everyone earned money by owning or working in factories. People moved to towns and cities to work in the new industries. This created a lot of new jobs in the cities, from shopkeepers to lawyers, who provided for the needs of the community.

Henry Ford (1863–1897)

Henry Ford built his first car in Detroit, Michigan, in 1896. His **assembly line** system was designed to mass produce cars like the Ford Model T. Each worker would fit one part of the car as it moved along the assembly line. This produced many more cars than if each worker was producing a whole car alone. This mass production meant that the Ford Model T could be produced cheaply enough to be bought by ordinary families.

An Assembly Line of the Ford Motor Company

What Has Changed Since 1900?

Nowadays, most women work outside the home in paid jobs. This was not the case in 1900, although more women were starting to earn money. The number of women working increased when many men went to fight in World War I between 1914 and 1918.

Changes in technology since 1900 have meant that fewer people work in factories today. Many factories also became cleaner and safer. New products like computers were made in different ways than the products of the Industrial Revolution.

During World War I, women took on many of the jobs that had traditionally been done by men.

Globalization

Since the late 1900s, work and earning money has changed because of **globalization**. Different parts of the world have become more closely connected than in the past. This is because of the growth of instant communication through phone and Internet. Air travel means that people and goods can move around the world more quickly. Many of the products that are bought in North America and Europe are now made in Asia and shipped to customers around the world.

The Internet and communications revolution have meant that many people can do their jobs from anywhere.

Larry Page and Sergey Brin
Founders of Google

The Google search engine is used by millions of people around the world to find information. Larry Page and Sergey Brin came up with the idea for the search engine while they were in college. The company was founded in 1998 and made its two founders into billionaires.

How Do People Earn Money Now?

Most people earn money by working for an individual or a corporation. They are paid for the work they do. The jobs that people do are normally divided into two main areas:

- Work that uses **natural resources** to create products that can be exchanged for money. This group can be divided into agricultural workers who grow food and other materials, and industrial workers who use **raw materials** like iron to make products.

- Work that provides services to others, including teachers and firefighters. These workers do not make a product, but they provide services that, in many cases, we could not live without.

Agriculture and farming

All of our food has to be grown and harvested from the world around us. The breakfast cereal you ate this morning was made from crops grown on a farm. Animals for meat also have to be fed and looked after on farms. Farmers earn money by selling the things they farm. Some may be sold directly to supermarkets; others will be sold to companies to be processed into food.

Improved farming methods and technology mean that only around two percent of workers in North America and Europe work in **agriculture**. In poorer countries, many more people are farmers, but many of these farmers only grow food or keep animals to feed themselves and their families.

Fair Trade Coffee

Many consumers try to buy things as cheaply as they can. Supermarkets and food companies try to pay as little as possible to the farmers that grow the product. Many farmers in **developing countries** are very poor and earn little money from their crops. If you buy products like coffee that are marked as "**fair trade**," this means that the farmers have earned more money for their crop. These products often cost more, but **consumers** know that the farmers earn a larger share of the money they pay.

Working in industry

Industry means turning raw materials into useful products. This ranges from mining materials such as coal to making highly complex products such as an aircraft. Construction workers earn money building houses and other structures like offices and roads.

Manufacturing

Most people who work in industry earn money by making the products that we use every day. This is called manufacturing. The **Industrial Revolution** led to people working in large factories, and many still do, but some manufacturing is done by highly skilled people in small workshops. Manufacturing workers may make finished products or parts that will be included in a bigger product, such as a car.

Many of the products we buy are made thousands of miles away. These clothes were made in China, where workers earn less money. This means that the clothes can be made more cheaply.

This car was designed and built in India. When it was launched, the company that made it said it was the world's cheapest car. Many Indian people could now afford a new car.

The Motor Industry

Industries change when technology develops and people want to buy different things. The city of Detroit, Michigan, was called "the Motor City" because so many cars were made there by Ford, General Motors, and Chrysler. Since the 1970s, this industry has declined as people bought cars from other countries. These cars were cheaper and used less fuel. This means that many workers who earned money in the automobile industry in Detroit have had to find work elsewhere.

Manufacturing is not the only area of industry. Many people work to convert, or change, raw materials into things that we use every day. They are things which we barely notice until they are not there. If you have ever been in a power outage, you know how different life can be without services such as electricity, gas, and water. Many people earn money making sure these essential products reach us, and by mining raw materials like coal and oil to provide us with energy.

High-tech industry

Some of the products made by people who work in industry have not changed for centuries. But products like computers, cell phones, and other "gadgets" are changing all the time. As well as making the products themselves, people are **employed** to design new models. There are also big teams of people whose job it is to **advertise** new products to consumers and make sure the products reach the stores where they will be sold. They will all earn money from the company that makes the product.

Who Made My MP3 Player?

Your MP3 player may carry the name of a well-known company, such as Sony or Apple. You would think that it was made in Japan or the United States. The people who invented, designed, and sold the product may be in one of these countries, but the parts were probably put together in a huge factory in China. The many different tiny parts that make up one MP3 player were made in different factories around the world.

New products are developed by people who work in R & D (research and development). These people invent and test the latest gadgets.

Technology

Technology is not just important in **high-tech** industries. All areas of industry try to develop new technologies so they can make things more easily and cheaply. The way that people earn money changes because jobs that used to be done by people can be done by computers.

Who Works in Services?

Most people in the modern economies of **developed countries** like the United States, Australia, the United Kingdom, and other European countries work in services. The total amount of **wealth** produced by a country is called the **Gross Domestic Product (GDP)** of that country. Much of the GDP of developed countries comes from services.

People who earn money in services do not make anything from **raw materials**. However, the economy could not function without the services they provide.

Think about the services you use every day. Your breakfast probably came from a store where people put it on the shelf and worked at the checkout. The driver who drove your bus to school provided a service. Your teacher at school is also providing a service, as are the doctors and nurses who would care for you if you were ill. There is a wide variety of people working in services. Some of them earn huge amounts of money every year; others earn very little.

Professions

If you are ill and go to see a doctor, you expect that doctor to be highly trained and know a lot about illness and how to cure it. Jobs such as doctors, lawyers, and teachers are sometimes called professions.

Doctors have to study for many years before they can call themselves a doctor. Because only the best students can become doctors, this and some other professions generally earn more money than jobs that do not require long training or special skills.

Doctors make decisions that can affect whether their patients will live or die. To get these decisions right, doctors need many years of training.

23

Banking and finance

One of the biggest service **industries** is banking and finance. Banks do more than give people a place to keep their money. They are important because they lend money to people to buy houses. Banks also lend money to businesses so they can **invest** more money to increase the size of the business. If companies have money to invest, they may expand their business and even hire more people.

Solve It!
Who works where?
Do you think these people work in agriculture, industry, or services?

- Coal miner
- Lumberjack (someone who cuts down trees)
- Printer
- Firefighter
- Fisherman
- Website designer

This chart shows the proportion of people **employed** in different areas of the services sector.

| Hotels, restaurants and leisure – 12% | Trade, transportation, utilities and stores – 22% | Banking and business – 22% | Education, health, and government – 37% |

Note: Other services account for 7 percent.

Banks have been in the news a lot in the last few years. After making some bad business decisions, many banks have had to borrow money from the government to stay in business. Governments have supported banks because they fear that if the public lost complete faith in banks they would remove all of their money. Then, most of us would be unable to borrow money for cars, homes, and school.

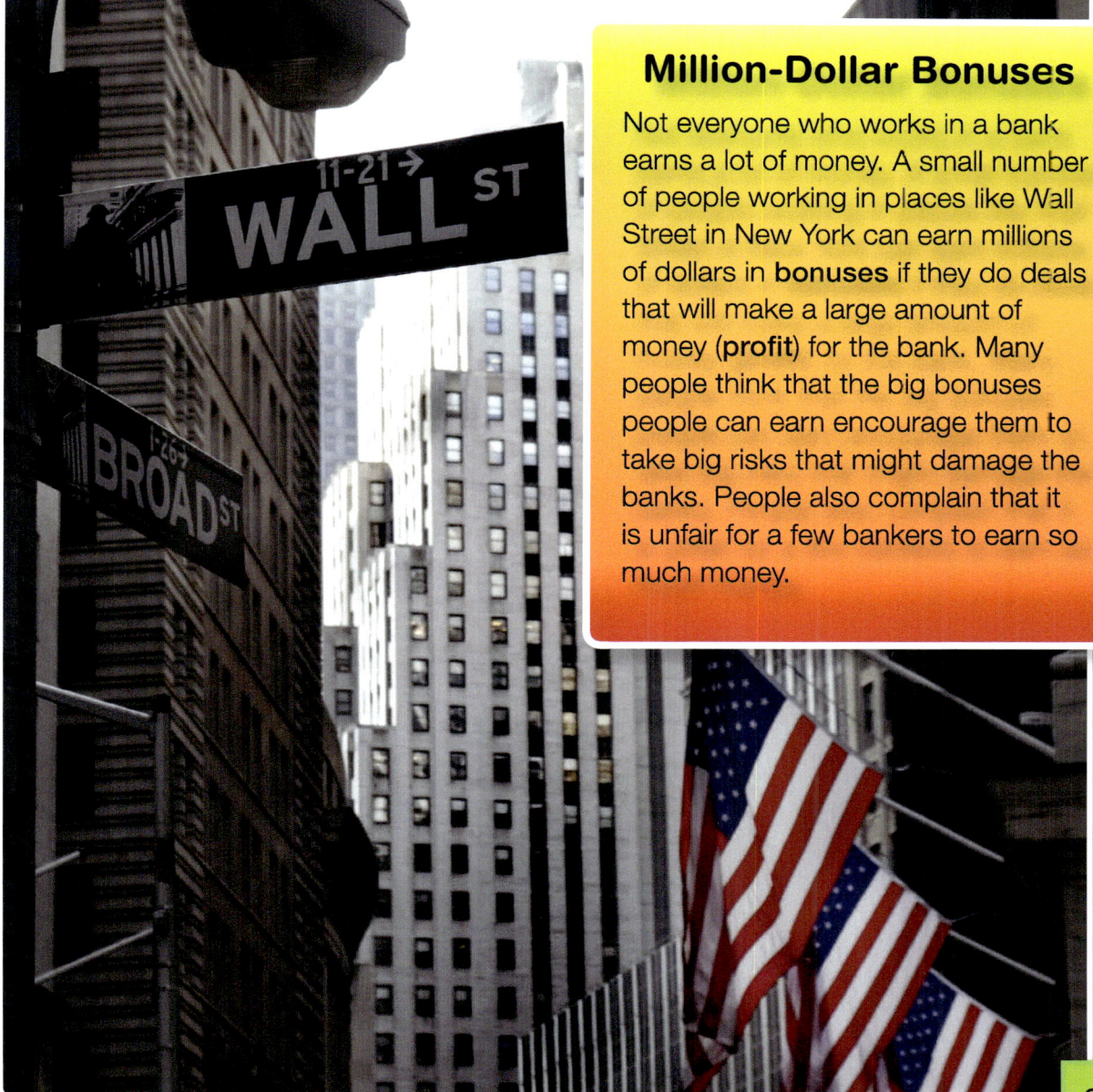

Million-Dollar Bonuses

Not everyone who works in a bank earns a lot of money. A small number of people working in places like Wall Street in New York can earn millions of dollars in **bonuses** if they do deals that will make a large amount of money (**profit**) for the bank. Many people think that the big bonuses people can earn encourage them to take big risks that might damage the banks. People also complain that it is unfair for a few bankers to earn so much money.

More people work for Walmart than any other private company. Asda in the United Kingdom is also part of Walmart.

Stores and restaurants

How many people work in your local store? If it's a small store, you might only see one person. There are many people who depend on stores to earn money. Bigger stores have buyers and managers who decide what the store will sell.

Hotels and restaurants also employ a lot of people. Those who work in hotels and restaurants often get very little pay. They expect to earn some money from tips. Customers will pay a little extra for their meal to reward good service.

Value of training

We saw earlier in this chapter that doctors are well paid because they are highly trained and have skills that are highly valued. Although there are many talented people working in stores and restaurants, they do not have to train for many years like a doctor. There are more people who could work in stores and restaurants so their **value**, or the amount they can earn, is lower.

Trade Unions

For most people, earning money depends on finding a company that will pay them for their work. If the employer does not need you to work anymore, or they can find someone who will work for less money, you may lose your job. Many workers group together in trade unions to bargain with employers. A trade union has more power to bargain than a single worker, because it speaks for all the workers. The trade union can call a strike, meaning that all employees will stop work and the employer will be unable to run its business.

How Do Public Workers Earn Money?

People who work for the federal or state government are said to work in the public sector. These people include government officials, also called the civil service, and the armed forces. Public school teachers are usually paid by the state in which they work. In many countries, like the United Kingdom, the government also pays doctors and nurses.

Teachers are not the only people who have to be paid in school. Think of all the other people who work in your school, from custodians to secretaries.

Paying taxes

The government can afford to pay all these people because everyone pays a proportion, or part, of what they earn to the government. This is called tax. Even those workers who are paid by the government have to pay tax. We all pay tax whenever we buy something in a store, since some of what we pay goes to the government.

Government spending is normally a big point for discussion during elections. If people do not like the way their taxes are being spent, they will vote for a new government. **Politicians** often talk about cutting spending. Some of the spending is on paying people, so this often means that people will lose their jobs.

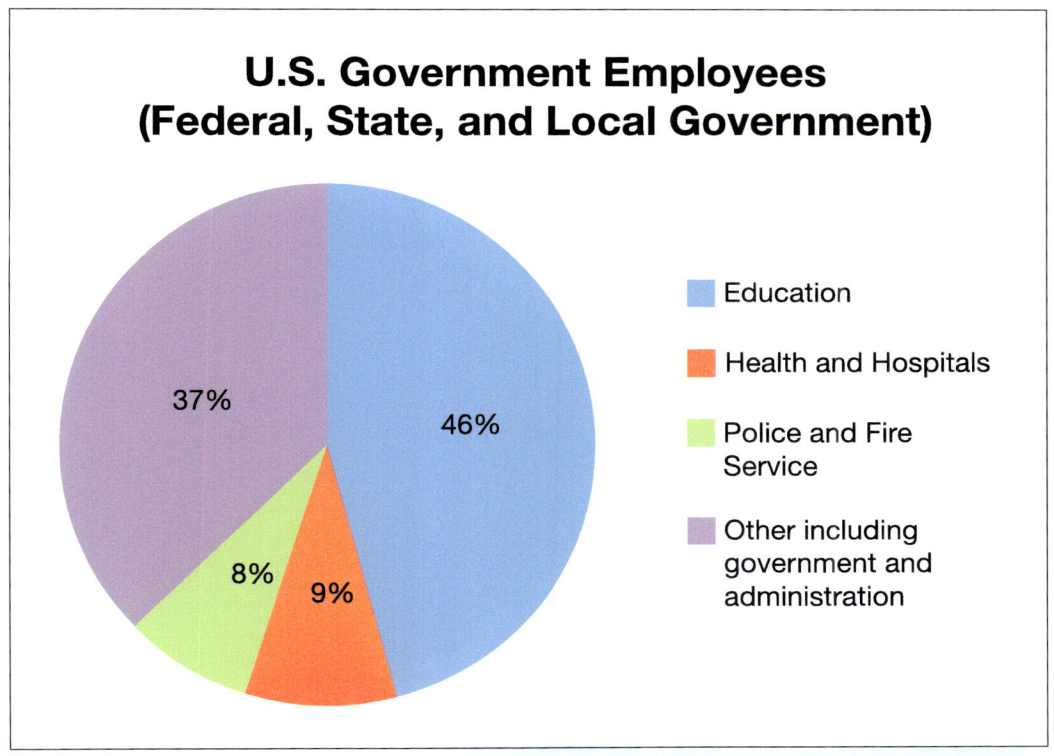

This pie chart shows the different jobs that are in the public sector. Areas where more people are employed will have a bigger section of the pie chart.

Does Everyone Work for Someone Else?

Not everyone earns money working for someone else. Many people start or run their own business. Most of these businesses are owned by a single person. They may have a particular skill, such as a plumber or electrician, or they may own a small store. People who run their own business enjoy the freedom of not having to work for someone else. However, the success of the business and whether they get paid at the end of the month depends on them and whether their business makes a **profit**.

All businesses start small

Even though most of these businesses are very small, all of the world's major corporations were at one time small businesses. Bill Gates and Paul Allen started Microsoft when they left college in 1975. By the year 2000, it was one of the world's largest companies. Many other **high-tech** companies have grown dramatically in recent decades as the Internet has changed many businesses.

Other ways to earn money include buying and selling property and **investing** in companies. These investments will hopefully rise in **value** over time. However, investments are risky and can lose value as well.

Madam C.J. Walker (1867–1919)

Madam C.J. Walker became the first African-American woman millionaire in the United States. She was the daughter of former slaves. She developed a product for straightening hair in 1905. Madam C.J. Walker's network of sales agents sold her products across the United States. She once said "... if I have accomplished anything in life, it is because I have been willing to work hard."

Who Decides How Much People Earn?

Although everyone needs to earn money, some people earn more than others. When you do paid work, you are basically selling your skill and the time you spend at work, just as if you were selling a product. The amount you are paid is your price, and this price is called a wage or salary. It will depend on how much people think your skills are worth.

Supply and demand

Wages, or the money earned from work, will be low for those jobs where there are many people who could do the job. Because there is a good supply of workers and the job does not require many special skills, employers do not have to pay high wages. The government sets a minimum wage that everyone should earn. Employers are not allowed to pay workers less than this amount.

The amount you can earn will rise if your skills are in high demand. This means that you have skills that are useful and cannot be easily found elsewhere. We have already discovered that doctors have skills that are in high demand.

Some jobs are particularly well paid because they require a talent that is in very short supply. Stars of sports, music, and entertainment are paid well because their talents are very rare.

Solve It!

Who earns more?
Which of these jobs do you think would be best paid? Why?

- Grocery store worker
- Bus driver
- Lawyer
- NFL football player
- Plumber

Airline pilots need many years of training. For this reason, the supply of airline pilots is limited and demand is high. This means that airline pilots have a high value to the companies they work for. But many airline pilots have received pay cuts because the airline industry has become less profitable in recent years.

What Happens When People Can't Earn Money?

At any time, there are a number of people in the economy who are not doing paid work. These people may have chosen not to work; they may stay at home to care for children or other family members. However, there are always people who would like to work but are unable to find a job. People who are not working but are looking for work are unemployed.

Unemployment

Television news reports will often say that **unemployment** has risen or fallen. When unemployment increases, this means that more people have lost their jobs than have found new ones. People can lose their jobs for many different reasons.

Outsourcing

Companies may decide that they cannot afford to pay so many people to make and sell their products. They may also try to save money by employing a separate company who will do the same work for less money. This is called **outsourcing**. Many American and British companies have employed **call centers** in India to answer calls from customers in the United States and United Kingdom.

Outsourcing call centers is made possible by advances in phone technology. Changing technology is another reason why people lose their jobs. There are many examples of jobs that existed in history that are no longer needed. When horses were the main means of road transportation, every village had a **blacksmith**. Nowadays, only a few remain.

A computer on every desk is a recent technological development. Before the 1990s, companies would employ many more typists to type up letters and documents that are now produced on computers.

People who have retired hope that their pensions will earn them enough money to enjoy their retirement.

Benefits

When people lose their jobs, they can usually claim some money from the government to make sure they are able to pay for essentials such as housing and food. This money will only be enough to cover essential costs until they are able to find work again. Benefits are also available for anyone who is unable to work because of disability or long-term illness.

Retirement

Most of us don't want to work for our whole lives. People who have worked for many years normally retire, or stop working, in their sixties. Once they retire, they will earn no more money from work so they will need to have some money saved for retirement.

People save money for retirement in different ways. Many people receive money from Social Security. Through social security, the government pays some people over age 65 a pension that provides some money. Other workers, such as those who work for the federal, state, or local government, receive a pension from the government when they retire. Other retirement income comes from money that people have saved throughout their working lives. They save this money in a retirement account, which **invests** the money in companies. Hopefully by the time they retire, the amount of money in the retirement account will have increased.

Solve It!

Thinking about pensions

Do you save money to buy things you want? Maybe you have a bank account where you save money. Can you think of some reasons why it is a good idea to save money for the future?

Why Does All This Matter to Me?

Hopefully this book will have given you more understanding of where money comes from and how it affects your family and friends. When you leave school or college, you will need to earn money of your own. We have seen that the economy is always changing. What are the opportunities going to be when you go to work?

Some ways of earning money have disappeared or changed dramatically; new jobs and industries will take their place. The growth of the Internet has led to major changes in the economy since the 1990s. Emerging nations like China and India have become more important. Make sure you know what's happening so you can make informed choices about how you earn money.

Earning Money Now

It can be difficult for young people to earn money. There are many laws designed to protect young people, but these can limit your options.

- Sell things that you no longer need, either at a garage sale or online. Make sure you get permission from an adult.

- Walk dogs for friends and family, or water plants and feed pets when family, friends, or neighbors are on vacation.

- Bake cookies and cakes and sell these at school or other events. Make sure that you have permission from the school.

Stay safe! Be very careful when dealing with strangers or meeting people online, who may not be who they say they are. Make sure an adult knows what you are doing and can go with you if you are meeting someone.

China is now a major part of the world economy. People who can speak Chinese are likely to be in demand in the United States and Europe.

How are you going to earn money?

When thinking about your own future career, you need to ask yourself a lot of questions. A rewarding career is not just about earning lots of money. There are many other things to consider.

Think about what you want to do and what you are good at. You might prefer to work outside, and this could lead you to a job in **agriculture**. You might want to follow a particular interest. Think about whether it is more important to you to earn lots of money or to do something that helps others.

Making the right choices and studying hard mean that you will have the most opportunities when you have to start earning money yourself.

Architects design structures, from small houses to skyscrapers and bridges. If you want to be an architect, you will need to study the right subjects at school and college.

People who work for charities do not usually earn a lot of money. However, helping others and doing a job you enjoy can be very rewarding.

Researching the World of Work

There are many places where you can find out more about different ways of earning money. Your school or public library will have lots of information about different careers. If you are interested in a particular career, you may know someone who does that job already who can tell you more about it. Many companies are happy for young people to experience what it would be like to work there.

IN FOCUS:
Who Are the Richest People in the World?

Carlos Slim

In March 2010, *Forbes* magazine named Mexican Carlos Slim as the world's richest man. Slim owns more than 200 companies, including Latin America's biggest cell phone company. Despite his estimated fortune of $53.5 billion, he lives in a modest six-bedroom house. Inside, the walls of the house are covered with fantastic works of art.

Oprah Winfrey

Oprah Winfrey is the world's best-paid entertainer. Oprah was born into **poverty** and had a difficult early life. The success of Oprah's TV talk show made her the first African-American female billionaire. Oprah has also produced and starred in films and publishes magazines. She owns homes across the United States. Her income in 2009 was estimated at $275 million by *Forbes* magazine.

Bill Gates

William H. Gates III is currently the richest man in the United States. He owes his enormous **wealth** to Microsoft, the company he founded and made into one of the world's biggest corporations. Previously the world's richest man, Bill Gates, alongside his wife Melinda, has donated much of his enormous wealth to health and education projects around the world.

J. K. Rowling

In 2009 the *Sunday Times* newspaper estimated J. K. Rowling's wealth at $728 million, making her one of the best paid authors of all time. Rowling wrote the hugely successful *Harry Potter* series of books, all of which have been made into movies. Her first book was written in cafés near her home in Edinburgh, Scotland, while her baby daughter was sleeping. Rowling has used her wealth to support many charities.

Money Facts

How do people earn money?

Percentage of people working in different sectors in selected countries

Country	Agriculture	Industry	Services
Australia	4%	21%	75%
Brazil	20%	14%	66%
China	40%	27%	33%
Ethiopia	85%	5%	10%
India	52%	14%	34%
Mexico	14%	23%	63%
UK	1.5%	18%	80.5%
USA	1%	20%	79%

Source: CIA World Factbook

What is the unemployment rate?

Percentage of people unemployed in selected countries

Country	Unemployment Rate
Australia	5.6%
Brazil	8.1%
China	4.3%
Mexico	5.5%
Poland	11%
South Korea	3.7%
UK	7.6%
USA	9.3%

Source: CIA World Factbook (Percentages are 2009 estimates — some based on data for urban areas only)

Solve It!

Hourly rates

Job advertisements will often say how much money you would earn on the job. Sometimes this is a figure for a year, but other times it will include pay per hour.

If a job pays $10 per hour, can you work out how much you would earn in a week? You need to know how many hours you would work in a week. Once you know this, you can find the answer. You could also work out how much you would earn in a month or a year.

Answers to Solve It!

Page 23:
The lumberjack and the fisherman work in agriculture. The coal miner and the printer work in industry. Firefighters and website designers are very different but both are jobs in services.

Page 32:
The football player would probably earn most. The lawyer would be next, although some top lawyers would earn more than a football player. Plumbers have skills that are in high demand so they would be next, followed by the bus driver who also needs special driving skills. Most grocery store workers are less well paid because their skills are easiest to replace.

Glossary

advertise to draw attention to products and services by presenting them on TV, radio, newspapers, or the Internet so people will buy more of them

agriculture growing crops or keeping animals to provide food and other raw materials

assembly line process in which a product, such as a car, is put together in stages with each worker doing one task

barter simple system of exchanging goods rather than buying and selling things for money

benefits can be any good or helpful outcome from an action. In the economy, extra things provided by a company as well as salary are called benefits. Government payments to people who are unemployed or on a pension are also called benefits.

blacksmith person who works with and shapes iron. Blacksmiths were important in history because they made shoes for horses, the main form of transportation before cars were invented.

bonus money that someone earns on top of their normal pay

budget plan of how an organization or person will spend money, or the act of making such a plan

call center office where people are employed to answer phone calls from customers

capitalist capitalism is an economic system that depends on people investing capital (money) to make and sell products. The people who invest money are called capitalists.

consumer anyone who buys or uses the products made by capitalists. We are all consumers.

developed country country where industry and the economy are fully developed. These are usually wealthier countries and examples include the United States, the United Kingdom, major European countries, Canada, Japan, and Australia.

developing country poorer country where the economy is not yet fully developed. Examples include many countries in Africa, Asia, and South America.

employ give someone a job, use their skill and time in return for payment

fair trade agreement that aims to provide more money to the producers of a product, particularly if they live in poorer countries

feudal system economic system common in medieval Europe where people would give the results of their work to the local lord. The lord would provide them with land and protection in return.

globalization development of a global economy

Gross Domestic Product (GDP) total of everything bought and sold in an economy during any year. GDP is used to measure how big an economy is.

guild association of craftsmen or merchants in medieval times

high-tech using the latest developments in technology, often computer technology

Industrial Revolution major change and development in the industry of a country and development of factories. This happened first in Britain in the 1700s, followed by other European countries, Japan, and the United States.

industry area of the economy concerned with making raw materials into useful products, for example using metals in manufacturing

invest use money in order to try to make a profit, for example, by investing it in a business

medieval time period in European history between 400 and about 1500 CE

merchant person who trades and sells goods

natural resource raw materials that occur in nature and can be used to make and sell goods and services; examples include oil, coal, and natural gas

outsource pay another company or individual to do something rather than doing it within your own business.

pension money that is paid to someone after they retire from working, either by the government or a company

plantation farm where crops like cotton and sugar are grown. In the past, these often used slave labor and many were located in the southern United States and the Caribbean.

politician someone who is elected to local, state, or national government

poverty not having basic needs met

profit money that someone who invests money gets back on top of their initial investment. Capitalist businesses aim to make a profit.

raw materials material that can be processed and refined into a different, more usable form

slave person who is the property of someone else and can be bought and sold. Slaves are not paid for their work. Slavery was banned in most places during the 1800s.

Social Security United States government program into which workers make regular payments and that provides money to retired people and those who are unable to work

trade union group of all the workers in a trade or organization to give them more bargaining power with employers

unemployment being without a paid job

value how much something is worth

wealth anything that is produced by work. Wealth is also used to mean money.

Find Out More

Books

Catel, Patrick. *Graphing Money*. (Real World Data). Chicago: Heinemann Library, 2010.

Murphy, Patricia J. *Earning Money*. (How Economics Works). Minneapolis, MN: Lerner Publishing, 2006.

Thompson, Gare. *What Is Supply and Demand?* (Economics in Action). New York: Crabtree, 2009.

Websites

http://www.socialstudiesforkids.com/subjects/economics.htm
This site has a lot of clear explanations of different aspects of economics.

Index

agriculture 16, 18, 40
Allen, Paul 30
armed forces 28
assembly line systems 13
automobiles 13, 19

banking and finance 24–25, 37
barter system 8
benefits 37
bonuses 25
Brin, Sergey 15
budgets 7

call centers 34
capitalists 5, 12
career planning 40, 41
China 18, 20, 38
cities 9, 13, 19
civil service 28
companies 15, 16, 17, 19, 20, 24, 27, 30, 34, 37, 41, 43
computers 14, 20, 21
consumers 5, 17, 19

demand 32
Detroit, Michigan 13, 19
doctors 22, 27, 28, 32

economy 4–5, 22, 34, 38
elections 29

factories 4, 11, 12, 13, 14, 18, 20
"fair trade" products 17
feudal system 10
Ford, Henry 13

Gates, William H. "Bill," III 30, 43
globalization 15
goods 4, 5, 6, 7, 8, 10, 11, 12, 15, 16, 20
Google search engine 15
governments 7, 25, 28, 29, 32, 37
Gross Domestic Product (GDP) 22
guilds 9

high-tech companies 20, 21, 30
hotels 27

India 34, 38
Industrial Revolution 12, 13, 18
industries 10, 12, 13, 14, 16, 18, 19, 20, 21, 38
Internet 15, 30, 38
investments 5, 24, 30, 37
laws 12, 38
loans 24, 25
lords 10

manufacturing 18, 20
Microsoft 30, 43
MP3 players 20

natural resources 16

outsourcing 34

Page, Larry 15
pensions 37
professions 22
profits 5, 25, 30

public sector 28
restaurants 27
retirement 37
Rowling, J. K. 43

safety 14, 38
savings 37
services 4, 5, 6, 7, 13, 16, 20, 22, 24–25, 27, 28
shipping 10, 15
slaves 9, 10, 31
small businesses 11, 18, 27, 30
Smith, Adam 11
Social Security 37
stores 20, 22, 27, 29, 30
strikes 27
supply 32

taxes 7, 29
technology 12, 14, 18, 19, 20, 21, 30, 34
tips 27
trade unions 27
training 22, 27

unemployment 34

wages 32
Walker, Madam C.J. 31
Wall Street 25
wealth 4, 5, 22, 43
Winfrey, Oprah 43
women 14
workers 5, 9, 10, 11, 12, 13, 14, 16, 17, 18, 19, 22, 24, 27, 28, 29, 32, 34, 37
world economy 5
World War I 14